OVERDOSE

A Mother's Journey from
Suffering to Empowerment

Kim Wilkinson

Tellwell Talent
www.tellwell.ca

ISBN
978-0-2288-6582-7 (Paperback)
978-0-2288-6583-4 (eBook)

In memory of my son, Tristin, July 24, 1997–November 14, 2019. My greatest teacher, and one of the most beautiful souls I have ever known. I am grateful for the journey, the lessons, the memories, and the ongoing divine guidance you continue to bring me. Thank you for waking me up and leading me to my life purpose and to living my best life.

Introduction

If I knew twenty-five years ago what I know now, I would have parented much differently. Is it too late? In some ways, yes. In other ways, no. You can't change your past. You can either learn from it, and when you know better you do better, or you can become a prisoner of it. Everything in life comes down to choosing consciously or unconsciously.

Conscious source or outcome
Pleasant
Love
Soul
Compassion
Acceptance
Trust
Feeling in control
Heal

Unconscious source or outcome
Unpleasant
Fear
Ego
Resentment
Judgement
Worry
Feeling out of control
Suffer

Your whole experience of life is determined by your belief system. What you believe, you perceive. Perception as I have come to know it is more like deception.

It is our experiences and our influences that create our beliefs, which then lead to our thoughts, actions, and outcomes. When we have a less than desirable outcome, we are quick to blame someone or something else for our shitty experience. The truth is: it is 100 percent our responsibility.

We have been conditioned to see life in such a specific way—an *unrealistic* way, I might add—that it becomes difficult to consider any other options. We become stuck, we settle, and we miss out on living an incredible life.

Three people can all be involved in the same experience at the same time, together, and there can easily be three different perceptions of what happened. The profound thing about this is that often no one is wrong! In their own minds, based on their past individual experiences and beliefs, what each experienced is their truth. Yet often in these situations, we recognize this as someone being wrong or needing to convince them to see it our way. We often get upset and angry, even resentful, in this situation. We can quickly become judgemental and fall into that unconscious approach to living life.

A simple example: If you and I were standing back to back and someone asked us to point to our left, we would be pointing in different directions; however, we are both right. Accepting that there can be more than one truth is where we often struggle. Acceptance is a big part of finding freedom.

When we start to understand this possibility and apply it to all other life experiences, our perceptions will change, our beliefs will change, and our experience of life will change.

Life is an interesting journey. The greatest awareness I have come to realize is just how unaware we are as humans. We come into this world not knowing fear, judgement, shame, or many other unpleasant emotions. We quickly become exposed to trauma, generational behaviours, and patterns, and become conditioned to think and respond in ways that create much more trauma later in life. Without a deeper understanding of this, one would not even realize that they were exposed to trauma or that they have been carrying around years of emotional baggage. If you are thinking, *I am so lucky, I had a great childhood*, think again. I thought the same thing, until I started studying trauma. It is easy to understand that big-T traumas can create a significant amount of grief. What most don't realize is that many of the emotional experiences in childhood that appear to be small can create core beliefs and behaviours that can lead to a significant amount of grief in adulthood.

Life is actually pretty simple, but we complicate the hell out it. Life is basically a series of experiences, one after another, that are either pleasant or unpleasant, and the key to living a great life is in how we deal with or manage those experiences. When trauma happens we have two choices: heal or suffer. That is it. It really is that simple: heal or suffer.

We all want a life full of good experiences; however, the contrast is necessary. How would we know good if we didn't know bad? How would we know happy if we didn't know sad? How would we know light if we didn't know dark? An important part about surviving life and living life well is to approach it with compassion, understanding, acceptance, and a ton of gratitude. I can truly say now that I am grateful for everything, even the shitty things. They brought lessons and opportunities. Most just don't take the time to look for them.

Although I won't share all the details of our family struggles, I will share enough for you to understand how things got to such deep suffering, and the challenges we faced trying to move through it.

I will also share how I learned to move through some of my life's most difficult situations with peace and gratitude, how I found empowerment, and how I learned to become the "mom.calm."

The mom.calm isn't an actual website, it is a unique reference that came from a song my son made up, and I adopted the term as a handle. Before doing all of this work, I was *not* a calm mom. I was stressed out, exhausted, angry, and sad. I felt utterly hopeless and often like a failure. Now most days I feel calm, confident, in control, joyful, and powerful, and I may even go as far as saying "enlightened." At the end of the book, you will find a link to the song that will explain it all!

My greatest tragedy has been my greatest gift. It has not only helped me to see the truth of my own life— including traumas I didn't realize I had—it has helped me heal, connect to my authentic self, and now I teach others to do the same.

What I didn't realize, and what most people don't realize, is the importance of attachment and authenticity for a child, especially in the first three years of life. As I mentioned earlier, If I knew twenty-five years ago what I know now, I would have parented much differently! You only know what you know. When you know better, you do better. I have gained an incredible amount of wisdom over the last few years, and I have much more to learn— we all do.

My hopes in sharing part of our story, and what I have learned, is that it will encourage more parents to parent more consciously. I truly believe we as a society can reduce the risk of mental health and addiction concerns if we can break these cycles of multi-generational trauma, learn to better manage our own emotional health, and teach our children to effectively manage their stress, traumas, losses, and emotions.

Having said that, this book is not just geared towards parents, this wisdom and these lessons can be life-changing for every individual on this planet. It is the path to healing our self and healing each other. It is the path to freedom.

Chapter 1

There is nothing as special as those early days with your newborn child. The love you feel is beyond words and like nothing you have ever experienced. That soft, sweet smell of a new little human. Perfect in every way. Their skin so soft, their delicate little features, tiny fingers and toes, and their eyes full of curiosity and innocence. You could stare at them all day. When you hold your child close and surrender deep into that unconditional love, nothing else in the world matters.

At some point you start to wonder, *What will they look like when they are older? What will their personality be like? What career path will they take? Whom will they marry? How many kids will they have?* and so on. We never wonder, *Will they experience anxiety, depression, or trauma? Will they fall into addiction? Will they become homeless? Will they die before I do?* We assume they will have a wonderful, healthy, and happy life, because that is what is supposed to happen.

This was my experience with both my first and my second child. My assumption could not have been more wrong. My daughter Cayley, my first born, still struggles with mental health concerns at age 28. Although she still struggles, she has so much strength and resiliency, and I am so proud of her. She is definitely much wiser and has more awareness and resources than I had at her age.

Tristin, my son, is my second child, born in July of 1997. I knew very early in his life that he was going to have a very specific purpose. It was clear he was an old soul. From the time he could talk he was like a little wise old man. He had a big heart and was an old romantic. He was the kid who, if you gave him a box of candy in the mall, he would share with every stranger that walked by. If he only got one candy himself, he didn't care, he loved to share.

He would often come up to me out of the blue, brush my hair away from my face or take my face in his hands, and say something like, "I love you, Mom, you are so gorgeous," then he would kiss me and take my hand and either kiss it or just sit and hold it. He was so sweet.

Tristin loved to make people laugh. From his silly faces to his made-up songs to his mannerisms, he brought so much laughter to those he loved and to strangers. I remember one Sunday, when he was about three and his sister was about five, I had taken them to one of the local clothing stores where we lived. Momma needed a new bra, so as I sifted through options, the kids stood close and it didn't take long for things to get oddly quiet, and then I heard Tristin's little voice: "Mom, look. They almost fit," followed by his cute uncontrollable belly laugh. I turned to look and there he stood with the biggest pair of blue granny panties I have ever seen pulled up over his clothes and almost to his chin.

It happened to be a Sunday and church had recently ended, and it seemed several elderly women had flocked to the store. I remember laughing but also trying to quickly get those panties off him before anyone noticed, and they kept getting stuck on the fastener of his sandals. It wasn't long until both kids were laughing hysterically. I finally got them off and we just left without making a purchase, as the laughter was unstoppable.

I used to have to check his backpack before taking him to the caregiver's home that provided childcare. One time I forgot, and when I picked him up, the childcare lady said, "One sec, I have to grab all those juice boxes, the package of wieners, and box of crackers that Tristin brought." I guess he planned on feeding everyone there.

He truly saw beauty in everything! I remember, about that same time, walking into my room one morning and he was lying on my bed watching *Labour and Delivery*, a birthing show on TV and it was quite graphic, clearly showing how a baby is born. I immediately wondered what crazy amount of questions were going to come from this. All he said was, "Aaaahhh, that's so cute," and he jumped off the bed and went to eat his cereal, no questions asked.

He had a similar response several years later when we were living on an acreage. My daughter was in 4-H and had sheep. When lambing season rolled around, Tristin was out in the pen, up front and centre for the live births, and he thought it was the most wonderful thing in the world.

He truly was non-judgemental and accepting of everyone, no matter what age, gender, race, or religion. For years I worked in swimming pools, and on weekends and during the summer Tristin would often come to work with me. He was not shy; he loved to swim and make new friends. Sometimes his "new friend" would be a small baby, sometimes it would be someone five years younger or older than him, sometimes it would be the eighty-plus-year-old man who liked to sit in the hot tub, and sometimes it would be another kid who didn't speak English. It didn't matter who they were, they were his new friend and he was happy to just be with them.

He was definitely a lover and not a fighter. He had the most beautiful white-blond hair that would ringlet at the back. He loved hugs and kisses and holding my hand, even into his adulthood. When he first started playing sports, specifically hockey, he was definitely more compassionate than competitive. Numerous times he would knock someone over accidentally, and rather than take off on a breakaway, he would stop and help them up. He did eventually develop a competitive streak in his teen years once he joined football.

Like most kids, there were times when he could drive you nuts! There were times of non-stop talking and typical brother-sister fights, but the more frustrating behaviours mostly showed up later in his childhood and early teen years, and more so after his dad and I separated. At that time I didn't understand the behaviours. This included things like angry outbursts and phone calls from him, crying and upset about things other people had said or done. Sometimes I would catch him in lies or suspect he was stealing things from family members. I think we get conditioned to think that this is normal behaviour. We are told the terrible twos will happen; we are told raising teenagers is difficult. I can now clearly see that these behaviours were a trauma response, a cry for help, a behaviour that was trying to meet a need that wasn't being met. It wasn't until much later in life that I would find this deep awareness and understanding. Now it all makes perfect sense.

You will come to learn that I have a strong belief that it was Tristin who led me into my practice of conscious living, energy healing, and to the work I do now. I believe a part of his purpose was to wake me up and lead me to my purpose. I actually believe it was a soul agreement we made coming into this lifetime.

Today, we hear a lot about "consciousness" and "waking up." I realize now that Tristin was trying to wake me up from the time that he could talk. As I reflect back on our journey together and all that we went through, it was him and everything we went through together that really brought me to this experience of feeling more conscious and aware.

When he moved from his crib to his bed, he used to wake me up every morning by tapping his pointer finger gently on my third eye and whispering, "Mom, mom." At the time I had no clue what a third eye was! I had not heard of reiki, didn't know much about yoga or meditation, and I would have laughed if you told me I would be doing what I do today. I still have these moments of revelation where I am reminded of something from his childhood that has such a significant meaning or connection to my present life. Even while writing this very book, I came across a photo of Tristin in the bathtub at about two years old. I had forgotten how he used to love lying down in the tub with the water covering his body, his ears submerged, just his eyes, nose, and mouth above the surface of the water. He would just lie there in stillness for several minutes. At the time, I thought he was just weird. However, as soon as that memory came to mind I immediately thought of the float tanks we see today, sensory deprivation tanks to bring relaxation into the body. These things weren't even heard of back them, but this is what he was doing. This awareness was mind-blowing for me. This young soul had so much wisdom, yet I couldn't see the simple lessons being taught right in front of my own eyes until much later, and more so after he passed.

All I can say is that I am truly grateful for that beautiful little boy waking me up to truth, to life, and to finding my purpose.

Chapter 2

On November 14, 2019, I received a phone call with the worst possible news ever. I had just returned home from teaching yoga and noticed I had a missed call. It was from my son Tristin's girlfriend. I listened to the voicemail. Her voice was full of overwhelming emotion. She was slightly hyperventilating and crying, and through struggled words she left a message saying, "Kim, it's Kaylee. Can you please call me back, it's about Tristin."

I was 99.9 percent sure what she was going to tell me. I called back right away and through her tears and staggered breathing she told me the news. Tristin had died. My heart physically ached like never before. I was in shock and had so many different emotions and sensations running through my body.

She explained to me that they had used drugs earlier that day and then took a nap. She woke up and he didn't. She tried to revive him, called 911. No one could save him. It was too late.

I have to say that, for about a year and a half before this day, I intuitively knew this was going to happen. I mean, I hoped and prayed it wouldn't, but deep down I had this knowing that someday my son would die of overdose, I just didn't know when. There were other close calls in the past with Kaylee and Tristin. They were previously able to revive one another with naloxone, but not this time.

My little boy, my only son, had died. He was twenty-two years old.

My heart hurt so bad. Kaylee and I spoke briefly. I was in a state of shock, even though I intuitively knew this day was going to come. You can never really be prepared for something like this.

I told her I would call her back and went to tell my husband the news. I remember sinking into my husband's chest as he hugged me, and all I could say was, "My heart hurts so bad." The rest of the night was spent calling family and gathering more information from police and Kaylee. I remember feeling so bad for her. To this day I can't imagine how she must have felt and what she went through, not only losing the person she loved right in front of her eyes, but then having to call his parents to tell them their son died. What a horrible thing for someone to have to go through.

As mentioned, I intuitively knew this was going to happen. The four years prior to his death was a roller coaster of mental health and addiction concerns, family struggles and incredible grief.

My husband is not Tristin's father. His father and I separated when Tristin was five years old, and my current husband and I started our relationship when our children were in high school. As I shared earlier, I also have a daughter, and my husband has four children from his previous marriage. It is no secret that divorce can be hard on children. Blended families can be a challenge. Parenting, in my mind, is the hardest job in the world.

It is hard to imagine anything more painful than the death of your child. I believe seeing them suffer is actually more painful.

In the four years prior to Tristin's death, there was a tremendous amount of both physical and emotional suffering. I also know that there are likely many things that I am not aware of, and maybe it's best I don't know. There was suffering much earlier than the last four years of his life. It just wasn't as noticeable, and perhaps I was also in denial.

Tristin graduated from high school in 2015. I knew at this time he had significant emotional challenges. At the time I was still quite naive and probably in denial about a lot of things, and I chose to think that he was starting a new "adult" phase of life, and that things would just get better.

In the fall of 2015, he got into some drug related trouble with the police. It scared him. I thought it was enough to scare him away from that lifestyle. I was wrong.

In February 2016, I was notified by a friend that there was a news report out that stated Tristin was wanted for a suspected crime. I couldn't believe it. It was not in his nature, and I could not wrap my head around this. I got a hold of him on his cell phone and convinced him to turn himself in.

After turning himself in, he spent some time in prison in Edmonton. He was lucky to eventually be released with no charges, no criminal record. He was in there for a few months. Weekly, I would go pick up his girlfriend at the time and take her to visit with me, then drive her back home. While he was in there, he suffered a bad human bite on his arm during a fight. It wasn't treated and became badly infected. It was shortly after that he was released, and he spent several days in and out of the hospital for IV treatment for infection.

Before he was released from the remand centre, his sister and I went to his court hearings. He was eventually releasable with bail and a list of conditions. The most difficult condition to meet for him was finding and confirming a supervised place to live.

My husband was an active RCMP officer, and with charges still pending for the suspected crime, not knowing who he was involved with, and if he owed money or to whom, coming to live at our place was not a great option. At the time, all of our other children were either living on their own or with other parents. Our work schedules were incredibly busy and demanding much of our time, but we managed to get him released and a safe place to stay.

He started to rebuild the relationship with my husband. My husband and I didn't start our relationship until Tristin was in high school, so they didn't know each other in a long-term child-step-parent relationship, but prior to this they had spent some time together on weekends, and we took a trip to Saskatchewan together to visit my family. It was a challenging relationship to build based on Tristin's history with drugs and armed robbery charges, even though they were dropped. We knew Tristin was running with a tough and violent crowd for a time. As a police officer, my husband was in a difficult position, and I am sure my son felt uncomfortable with it too.

Despite the challenges in their relationship, they both seemed to have an understanding, and a respect for each other. I know Tristin thought very highly of my husband, and I know my husband really wanted Tristin to have a better chance at life and understood why Tristin did some of the things he did.

Shortly after Tristin's release from the prison, all charges were dropped, and not long after that I got a call from my son one evening around 1:30 a.m. It was winter, and he was crying and high (I didn't know at the time, but I suspected). He had a knife on him, he had become homeless with nowhere to go, and he was threatening to kill himself.

I drove forty-five minutes from where I lived to go pick him up and take him to the hospital. I knew I needed to get him mental health support.

It broke my heart to see him suffering so badly. We were in a private room in the emergency department. The lights were off, and just the light from the hall peeked through. He was likely high on I don't know what, but it was clear he was in a deep, dark place. He couldn't stop sobbing and kept mumbling words about being useless, that no one cared, and that he wanted to die. The nurses were impatient and rude. I am sure they were tired of seeing people come into the emergency department in the same state as Tristin, but I couldn't help but feel like their energy said, *Here is another stupid kid wasting our time.* I felt so helpless. I was polite and patient. I tried to get him assessed, and asked for him to be admitted to Alberta Hospital. I was truly worried about him having suicidal thoughts. By this time he was eighteen, an adult. This made things even more difficult.

We spent the night and part of the next day in emergency, and I spoke to anyone and everyone I could to get him help: the Alberta Alcohol and Drug Abuse Commission, mental health services, shelters. My son needed a safe place, professional help for addiction, and professional help with trauma recovery. To my surprise, I was told he did not meet requirements to have an assessment done to be admitted to Alberta Hospital. My initial response was, "Are you fucking kidding me? I picked him up in the middle of the night in a park, homeless and with a knife, and he is threatening to kill himself, and he doesn't qualify for an assessment to be admitted into a psychiatric hospital?"

I felt let down by our health care system, and I think Tristin felt completely defeated.

I had hoped that the experience of being in prison would be enough for him to be able to turn his life around. At the time I didn't understand the severity of the root of his suffering, which was leading to all the behaviours and unhealthy choices. I also didn't understand how easily a person gets sucked down into that spiral of continuous deep pain and suffering.

I didn't know then, but I can tell you now: when people get caught in that spiral, the pain is unbearable. They become full of guilt and shame, and they often lie, steal, and display other harmful behaviours. It is not done consciously or intentionally, although it may appear that way. It is a trauma response. I got to know these patterns and behaviours very well in the last few years Tristin was alive. Although it took me a while to truly understand it all (and not fully until after he died), I seemed to have this understanding that it was not his fault and I had compassion for him rather than anger or resentment. It is easy to think the person is choosing it or that they can just stop if they want to. It is not that easy. I can tell you that the world is full of hurt people. There are no bad people, there are hurt people and hurt people, hurt people.

For a time, I did have hope and believed he was changing—again, I may have been in denial or just unaware. We got him off the streets and living with his sister in our rental house. He started a part time job, and he had a desire to change. Right before Christmas 2016, he lost the job. He had been there a few months. He told me he got laid off, but I suspect otherwise. I always just accepted what he said, even though I had a strong belief he was lying. What was done was done, and there was no use starting big arguments about it.

He ended up going out of town for a few days right before Christmas. He told me he was doing some work for a friend's dad. I didn't believe him. My intuition told me it was another lie, but again, it wasn't worth getting into a big argument about it, and by that time he was over eighteen, an adult making his own choices. I had to accept that.

He was supposed to come to our place for Christmas and celebrate with the family. Twenty-one of us gathered, including the rest of our children, some aunts and uncles, and one of the grandparents. Although there had been a significant amount of tension within the family as a result of various struggles with mental health and addictions, we were on an upswing, and again I was hopeful that we could come together as a family and find support and acceptance for one another.

I kept calling him the few days before Christmas, asking when he was coming back to the city. He said he would be back in time for Christmas. He called me on Christmas Eve crying, saying he got jumped and received four stab wounds, and the palm of his hand got burned. He texted the pics to me and I still to this day can't find words to describe how I felt. Again, I suspected the story he told me was not the truth. He said he and a friend were out walking to go grab a bite to eat and got jumped and stabbed. He said they ran back to his friend's place and that he accidentally put his hand on a hot stove in the garage when arriving there. I didn't question him on his story. It had already happened, and nothing was going to undo the damage done. What was important was that he get appropriate medical attention.

There was absolutely no way he could join us for Christmas. It would have been a huge trigger for many family members, and he was in no condition to do anything. After getting medical attention, he went back home to our rental place and sadly had to spend Christmas Day there alone.

Chapter 3

It was that Christmas Day (2016) when I experienced a big shift. By this point I had already started my emotional healing journey by applying what I had learned thus far from yoga teacher training, meditation teacher training, energy healing certifications and the many books I had read on personal growth and development. Sadhguru, Eckhart Tolle and Dr. Joe Dispenza were very influential and inspiring in my life at the time.

I decided to tell the family that Tristin would not be joining us for Christmas, as he was not in a good place mentally and he felt it best to just stay away. It broke my heart. I was sad that he had been hurt physically and emotionally; I was angry that he had chosen to put himself in the situation. I suspect the whole thing was drug-related. I can't say for sure, but I have a pretty good understanding of trauma, addictions, and behaviours related to this lifestyle now, so I am pretty certain it was drug-related.

A few times on Christmas Day I just stepped into another room, put my hands on my heart, closed my eyes, and allowed myself to really feel the energy of the emotions swirling around within me.

I reminded myself that what was done could not be undone, that I had no control over anyone or anything outside of myself, and that all I could really do was to make the best of that day and deal with the next day when it came.

I remember physically feeling the emotion in my body move from my stomach to my chest back to my stomach and throughout other areas of my body, and then it subsided. In that moment what came into my mind was, *Calm in chaos*.

I realized that even though I felt like I was in a place of suffering, I felt empowered. I realized in that moment that life can be falling apart around me but I can choose to create calmness within.

I didn't cry that day. It wasn't because I wouldn't allow myself to or that I was distracted from it, which most of us are taught to do. I found the path to freedom from suffering. I also believe I was becoming more resilient.

It was then that I realized that I needed to further explore and share this, and teach this to others.

On Boxing Day I took leftovers to Tristin. I took him to the hospital three times that day for IV antibiotics and dressing changes. He had to go three times a day for another three days. The only family members who knew about what had happened and why Tristin really didn't join us for Christmas at the time was my daughter and my sister-in-law and brother-in-law. They were quite aware of his struggles, as there was a time prior to that when they had gone to check on Tristin for me. I can't remember exactly when or where I was, but I was teaching or doing something that was difficult to get away from. My daughter had tried calling me, and then texted a message saying Tristin was in a really bad state and was talking about killing himself. He was living with her at the time in our rental house. I was terrified and desperate for help. Thankfully, they went over and were able to have a talk with him and calm him, and the situation resolved positively.

You may be wondering why I reached out to them rather than my husband. My husband had a significant amount of his own stress during this time, and I felt sharing all of the struggles with him would have had an even greater negative impact on him and our relationship. I told him about everything that happened about six months later. At the time I felt handling it on my own without my husband was the best decision.

We made it through the holidays, and, going into the new year, I convinced Tristin to go to an addiction treatment centre. Through much research and reaching out to community organizations, we finally found an opportunity! We applied for him to participate in a ninety-day treatment program, and he started on February 14, 2017.

I remember we went to a local restaurant for breakfast first thing that morning and then I drove him to the treatment centre. I visited him regularly, and he would come spend the day with us on Sunday passes. I was so proud of him. I was always proud of him. Even though I didn't agree with many of his decisions and actions, I sort of understood them. I knew he wasn't himself, but that my sweet baby boy was still in that young adult body. After his ninety days of treatment, I saw that sweet little boy I hadn't seen in a long time. I remember his ninety-day counsellor telling me that underneath the anger, the sadness, and the tough-guy act, he realized there was just this young boy inside who wanted to be loved, to belong, and to have fun.

One of the most painful experiences was watching him suffer from verbal emotional abuse. I remember him coming to our house for the day on a Sunday pass. While he was there, he made a phone call to someone he loved, wanting to share his excitement in the progress he had made and hoping for support, acknowledgement, and maybe some more encouragement. The response from the other end came in the form of yelling, commenting that he didn't need treatment, he needed to get a job. Although not on speaker phone, I could clearly hear the conversation from across the room. This person was yelling "I love you" and "stop being a disappointment" in the same sentence. I remember this so clearly. It broke my heart seeing him sitting on the couch and sobbing his heart out while being yelled at. It went on for at least fifteen minutes. Several times I whispered for him to hang up, saying he didn't need to put up with that. He couldn't do it; he just kept trying to explain and kept getting yelled at more.

I eventually started recording from my phone, as I couldn't believe how horrible it was. I still have the recording. I can't bring myself to listen to it, and I can't bring myself to delete it either.

I can't imagine what Tristin was feeling, but it broke my heart. I can still feel the heaviness in my chest, the heat on my face, and the turning of my stomach when I think back to that day, seeing him hurting so badly. Once again, I found myself feeling helpless.

It is hard to support others when we don't agree with their choices and behaviours. I know now there are times where I was not meeting Tristin's needs, but I never yelled at or belittled him. I can tell you that, back then, I didn't understand enough to be able to support him in the best way possible, but I did know that compassion and patience were important for anyone trying to better themselves.

I attended his treatment program graduation. I had a group of amazing friends join me there to celebrate with him. It was such an amazing day and he was so happy, so proud, so motivated. I was happy too, and so proud of him. I helped him get set up in his own place and got him a bed and a phone. I tried to encourage and motivate him, but I also told him that if he went back to old ways, I would not be able to help him financially like that again. I was maxed out. He understood. I still didn't quite understand the power of trauma and a (addiction) ddiction at this point, so I didn't realize that there was a high risk of relapse.

Chapter 4

Tristin quickly got a job, a great opportunity as a pipe-fitter apprentice. It happened so fast. I remember he made a post on Social Media about looking for work as a pipefitter and someone messaged him, told him to get the required safety tickets and head to Fox Creek, Alberta, ASAP. It was such a whirlwind. I remember driving him to his two-day course to get his safety tickets, and messaging friends and posting on Social Media in between, trying to find him a place to stay.

Somehow things all fell into place. We got him up there, he started working, and he was loving it.

As quickly as he got that job, he relapsed and lost it. While he was there he met his girlfriend Kaylee, the one who would eventually tell me he had died.

It was a roller coaster for them trying to get out of the cycle of addiction. At one point they ended up moving to Edson, Alberta, which is two hours from Edmonton. Tristin had come to the city a few times so I was able to see him. I knew he was using again. I had learned the behaviours and patterns by this point: communication would be sporadic and he would message asking for money. I knew I couldn't enable him. When I saw him, I would buy him food or get him clothes. I knew if I gave him money it would just go to drugs, and honestly I just didn't have much money to give. When he would be in the city for a few days I would let him borrow my Tablet. He would always forget to log out of his various social media accounts, and I would read some of it, just enough to confirm my suspicions that he was using again, then I would log him out. As a mother there are some things you don't need or want to know!

I knew I had no control over his life. He was almost twenty. All I could do was try to encourage him and pray to God he would get help.

There was a part of me that truly believed that at some point he would overcome the addiction and live the life he truly wanted. Out of all of our children, he is the one who most wanted to get married and have a family. He would have been a great dad.

There was also that part of me that intuitively knew this would take his life. I prayed it didn't, but I knew it would. I just didn't know when.

After moving to Edson, Tristin started to suffer from several medical concerns. He often had chest pain. He had anxiety and trouble sleeping. He had a scare with testicular cancer and seemed to be taking many more prescribed medications.

As a result of all the years of stress and trauma and the various drugs he had put into his body, he eventually developed two softball-sized tumours that were putting pressure on his heart and lungs, hence the chest pain and trouble breathing. He needed to have surgery. I found out afterwards that he was so terrified that he didn't show up for his first scheduled surgery. I convinced him to contact his doctor and ask for it to be rescheduled. He finally did, and I picked him and Kaylee up and drove them to the hospital. I was very frustrated that day, and later felt terrible for being so impatient and frustrated. He was terrified to have that surgery. I wish I had been more compassionate toward him that day. I remember telling him I loved him and hugging him, but I was also a bit short with him. One thing Tristin was always bad for is waiting until the last minute to call to ask for a ride somewhere. I never minded driving him, but it would often not give me enough time to get my work covered or adjust my schedule so I could. This was the case when he needed a ride for his surgery. It was a last-minute request for a ride, so I quickly adjusted my schedule but felt very frustrated. Nevertheless, I got him there with Kaylee and he had his surgery.

I visited him in the hospital. He told me (after his surgery) that he was so scared that he took a ton of illegal drugs before going into surgery. I was surprised they operated and even more surprised that he was still alive at that point, especially after finding out he had so many illegal drugs in his system on top of the drugs required for surgery.

His surgery was invasive. There was a large incision down the upper-left side of his back and another that went from the middle-outside of his back and wrapped around to his abdomen. They had to cut several ribs to be able to access the tumours to remove them. He had many staples and was badly bruised. He was in a lot of pain. He had such a high tolerance to drugs at this point that, no matter what they gave him, it didn't help.

 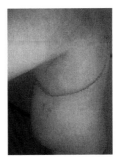

He was released within a few days and moved into a basement suite he arranged to rent from a friend of his. I can't remember where Kaylee was at this point; she may have gone to Kelowna for treatment. The few years prior to all of this had been such a roller-coaster. I had my own traumas and grief, On top of everything with Tristin, I had my own traumas, grief and unresolved emotional experiences I was trying to deal with and was not having much success. I felt stuck in suffering. Somewhere in the middle of it I ended up with a concussion, which created significant physical and emotional suffering for about a year and a half. I will explain more about the concussion later in the book.

In some ways the things that happened are so clear, but sometimes I can't remember the order of events. It was like riding a roller coaster in a cyclone. It was exhausting.

Not long after his surgery, Tristin decided to go back to treatment and was able to quickly get into the place where he completed his ninety-day treatment program. We hadn't spoken for a bit, but he called me and told me he was there. I was pleasantly surprised, and I actually thought maybe that was it. I mean, after such an overwhelmingly intense surgery and the fear he was going to die from it, maybe this would be the turning point.

I visited him again during his second round of addiction treatment. Little did I know that would be the last time I would see him in person or hug him.

Chapter 5

During that last visit with Tristin at the treatment centre, he asked me if I would go to his storage unit and grab the few things he had there. He had assured me there were just a few things, but he needed them out so he didn't have to pay rent for another month. Again it was a short notice request, but I agreed to do it. He gave me the key, and the next day I went to the unit and discovered there was much more there than he had suggested. There were at least three truckloads. I had to work that day and didn't have time to make three trips, and certainly had nowhere to put all of his stuff. Our house was full, including the basement and the garage.

I decided to leave it there, and I emailed him to explain the situation and to see if he wanted me to contact the rental company. I would have paid the month for him, I just needed to know what he wanted me to do. Email was the only way to communicate with him while he was in treatment. He could call me on certain days, but I was not able to call him.

He got upset and sent me a nasty email back. It was frustrating and hurtful, but I also knew that he was likely struggling with a variety of things. He had needs and expectations and I was not able to meet them. He said he didn't want to talk to me again. I remember replying and telling him that I was sorry that he felt that way, that I truly wanted to help him, and that he was allowed to feel whatever he was feeling. I told him I loved him, and I was always a phone call or email away if and when he was ready to talk to me again.

I knew he would contact me at some point, and he did. I remember it clearly and I still have the message. He sent me a message on Social Media and told me that he had moved to Kelowna, and that he and Kaylee were going to have a fresh start. She had gone to treatment too, he was working, and he loved it there.

I was so happy to hear from him. I was happy to hear how happy he was. He was back working out at the gym and eating healthy, and that little sliver of hope came back for me: maybe he would make it.

For several months after that we talked on the phone and messaged back and forth, and then the old patterns of behaviours returned.

I would message him, and I could see that he received and viewed it, but he wouldn't respond. A few days later I would get a message back asking to borrow money. I wasn't the only one he would ask. My mom would often message me saying Tristin asked her for money. I quickly realized he was likely using again. We continued to stay in touch, at times through phone calls, others through text. His response time became longer and longer—days, sometimes weeks.

I used to get frustrated, as sometimes I would miss his call, and when I would call back I would not get an answer. I also made sure to tell him I loved him, that I believed in him, and that I was proud of him.

I had started to learn a lot more about emotional healing during that last year, and often tried to share inspirational books and videos in hopes of helping him.

I started to teach him meditation, gave him books to read to help with personal healing and growth, and tried to motivate him and encouraged him to get professional help. I did reiki sessions on him to try to reduce his anxiety. I helped him a bit financially, although not much, as I couldn't afford to.

The truth is, you can lead a horse to water but you can't make it drink. I also learned at this point that the more you "should" someone, the more you are met with resistance. Let go of what you can't control.

Chapter 6

I now understand that his trauma was creating his behaviours and his resistance to getting help and to stop using. He likely was still not feeling safe, loved, or heard. He carried blame and like many in his situation, shame, and that can put someone into protection mode, isolation, or dissociation, and me "shoulding" him was likely taking away any sense of control or power he had over his life.

What most people don't see when it comes to addicts or alcoholics, and what took me a long time to see and understand, is that it all stems from trauma. We have all experienced trauma; we all have unresolved grief and unresolved emotional experiences, because all we have been taught is to avoid and distract. It is taught during our upbringing, and it is reinforced through movies, TV shows, songs, and society. If you pay attention to it, you will notice that the "avoid and distract" messaging is everywhere! The messaging we see and hear on TV and in songs is, "drink to celebrate, drink to numb the pain, drink because it is the weekend, drink because it's summertime." If alcohol no longer numbs the pain, then drugs are often the next choice. It might start as prescription medication that a person eventually builds a tolerance for, and they need something stronger to continue to numb the pain. We have become a pill-popping society, and it is easy to be labelled with a condition and given a legal drug to resolve the symptoms. The truth, and the problem, is that it doesn't resolve the root cause. Tristin got his fair share of prescription drugs, but what he didn't get enough of was support, the right support, for healing the trauma.

Tristin fell into the world of addiction because of trauma and unresolved grief from his childhood and early adult years. We don't realize the impact some of the things we say and/or do have on our children. We don't realize the impact society, social media and social environments have on our children. We don't realize what we are teaching them with our own actions. As a parent, you think you know everything that your kids go through. I can assure you, you don't.

We don't realize that there are things that happened to our children we were never told about. Did you tell your parents about everything that happened to you? When a client in a therapy session is asked, "Who did you talk to?" after disclosing an emotional event, nine times out of ten the answer is "no one." A child should feel safe and comfortable to talk to their parent about anything, and when they don't it is a result of some other past emotional event between the child and parent. I especially realized this during this past year working with my own clients and reflecting on my own childhood. Many of my trauma teachers have explained that there is often, if not always, trauma that has happened prior to the trauma that has been identified. For example, a child may not want to tell their parent they were bullied at school. The bullying is often seen as the traumatic event, but there was a previous traumatic event that has made that child not want to disclose the bullying to the parent. It may be because in the past the parent brushed something similar off, or made a comment like, "Don't be a baby, stand up for yourself," or just ignored the child. If the child doesn't feel safe and supported, or doesn't feel like they have been heard or validated, they will often supress the emotions.

My husband, who is a police officer, knows the world my son fell into all too well from a different perspective. He knows the risk to safety, the violence, and the crime involved. While my husband is one of the most understanding and compassionate men I know, the world Tristin was caught in was likely a huge trigger for my husband. His primary concern was safety for our family. Not knowing who Tristin was involved with, who he might have owed money to, and how much are things that put us or could have put us at great risk over the years when he was in active addiction. During this time my husband worked a file where a guy was murdered because he owed $100 to a drug dealer. While there were times when I thought the best thing for Tristin would have been for him to come live with us, I also knew that it could have been very dangerous. The whole situation was so complicated.

We really had to be careful about how we managed the entire situation, and it created a significant amount of tension and challenge in our marriage and within our other family relationships.

I was often worried about finances and felt like I never made enough or didn't contribute enough to our marriage. I remember seeing a painting at a local massage clinic; it was a fairly large canvas of splatter art, and the sale price was $6500. It was beautiful and there was no disrespect in my mind, but I remember saying to myself, *I could do that and sell it for a quarter of the price and still make some good money.* So I took up painting, the very thing that led to the concussion I previously mentioned. I had never painted in my life, but I had a strong pull to start. I quickly started to sell my paintings for $40, $75, $250, and as high as $800. I didn't recognize it at the time, but it was my distraction from dealing with my pain. It became *my* addiction. It was my thing to do to keep busy, pass the time until things got better. The truth is we are all addicted to something that numbs our pain. If it is not drugs or alcohol, it's food, shopping, sex, gambling, social media, or other compulsive and repetitive behaviour.

Addiction is addiction. Some medical experts will argue addiction is only related to drugs or alcohol.

Dr. Gabor Maté, a trauma/addiction expert and one of my ongoing teachers, says, "Addiction is not a choice that anybody makes, it is a response to human suffering, it is any behaviour that gives temporary relief from suffering."

The only difference is that drugs and alcohol have a much more harmful impact on the body physically and physiologically than some of the other choices of behaviours.

By this point I had a consistent spiritual practice and I believe the universe kept giving me signs to deal with the truth, and when I didn't listen, the signs got louder and stronger. It started with lights flashing on and off in our kitchen, things falling off shelves, and the rear-view mirror in the vehicle randomly falling off while driving. I kept ignoring the signs.

Then that one day, when painting on the biggest canvas I had ever done, both feet went out from under me and I fell. I first landed on my right butt cheek then fell back, hitting the back of my head on the basement floor. Fortunately I did not lose consciousness, but I certainly had a terrible headache and other concussion symptoms. It left me in a terribly emotional and depressive state for over a year, along with extreme headaches. On top of dealing with all the family stress and financial worries and worrying about Tristin, my concussion had me spiralling into a deep depression.

During that first year after the concussion, I would just break down and cry anytime, anywhere, and for no apparent reason. I would be driving to the grocery store and just start crying. Driving was another thing that was affected. There were days when I would be driving to teach yoga, the same place I have been teaching for years, and halfway there I would suddenly forget how to get there. I would eventually remember, but that one to two minutes when I didn't know was a terrifying feeling.

I had a hard time sleeping. I developed severe anxiety. I was given medication for it but could never bring myself to use it much. I didn't like the after-affects of taking the medication. My headaches were so bad that every six to eight weeks I would have to get injections in my head (basically novocaine) to numb the pain, so my brain could relax and start to heal. When I would go for these injections, it was always sixteen to twenty-eight needles into the top, sides and/or back of the head, into the scalp.

I can't even begin to explain the pain of needles going into your scalp. It would help, but it was the most physically painful thing I have ever felt. It would numb quickly, and once I was done I would barely make it to the parking lot before I would burst into tears. I think it was mostly my body's way of releasing all the built-up emotional energy. I would cry for a minute or two and then feel much better. My husband used to have to drive me. As time went on and I got used to them and less emotional, I would drive myself. I would still often have a little cry in my car before driving home. It was really difficult during this time not being able to do what I knew I needed to do for my mental health. Yoga, Meditation and Reiki energy healing were things I practiced and taught. I had several other tools to help calm anxiety, clear my mind, improve my sleep, etc., but I was in such an emotional funk I could not bring myself to do the work, and so I suffered. I stayed in a place of suffering for almost a year.

It is no secret that first responders are often affected by occupational stress injuries, post-traumatic stress disorder, and other mental health concerns. I am still to this day amazed by my husband's resiliency considering the significant amount of trauma he has been through and exposed to, but nevertheless, there is still trauma. We all have it. Again, most of us misunderstand trauma and don't realize how much of it, along with unresolved grief, we have.

During this four-year struggle, Tristin was struggling to deal with his lifetime of trauma. I was struggling to deal with my lifetime of trauma, my husband had his own lifetime of trauma he was trying to deal with, and my daughter had hers as well. None of us could support each other in the ways that we needed, not because we didn't want to, but because we didn't know how. We were all triggered and could barely take care of ourselves, never mind each other. Along with our big-T traumas, we all had basic human needs that were not being met, and that kept us stuck in a state of chaos.

Some of our basic human needs are the need to feel safe, the need to feel loved, the need to feel heard and the need to belong. When these needs are not met, a person can experience trauma. This can often lead to (unconscious) behaviours that attempt to meet those needs and are often not the best choice of behaviour. We were all trying to get through them unconsciously, needing the support of each other and not being able to support each other or meet each other's needs.

Most of us aren't taught how to deal with stress, trauma, grief, and loss. We are taught to keep busy, give it time, be strong, and so on. Most of us can barely manage our own emotional health, how do we teach our children to do so? The cycle of "avoid and distract" continues. It becomes multi-generational trauma.

It was so painful to see Tristin suffer so much, physically, mentally, and emotionally. During his last few years of life, I watched and listened to him cry more than laugh. It made me so incredibly sad. I felt helpless. I just wanted him to be happy.

My saving grace through this challenging time in life was my spiritual practices: yoga and meditation and the knowledge I was gaining by diving deep into a variety of personal development books, programs, and trainings. I will share more about the specifics of my practices later on.

Chapter 7

I had actually started my healing journey long before Tristin passed away. Looking back, it was like God, or the Universe, was preparing me to deal with the struggles that were to come. More so now, I look back and I believe that this all stems from a soul agreement made by Tristin and I to find my life purpose. I spent the first twenty years of my career working in the corporate world, a manager in municipal government. I was always a teacher of some sorts on the side, mostly fitness and swimming pool operations. If someone would have told me I would be a yoga/meditation teacher, a reiki master, and a grief & trauma recovery coach I would have laughed and likely said something inappropriate.

I mentioned at the start of this book that, when Tristin went from sleeping in a crib to a bed, he used to wake me up daily by tapping his little finger on my third eye and whispering, "Mom, mom." Back then I didn't even know what a third eye was, but I can tell you the journey of being his mom for twenty-two years woke me through various levels of consciousness and he continues to wake me up consciously, just in new ways.

By the time my sweet boy's life came to an end, as heartbreaking as it was, I had a deep awareness, an understanding, and some incredible tools and resources to navigate my grief and to heal from my loss. I would not have all of this if it weren't for the experiences that he and I went through. There is much more to his story, but there is enough here to grasp a good understanding of the struggle we went through as a family.

When Tristin died, I knew I had two options: heal or suffer. Nothing will ever bring him back. Suffering would only continue to hurt myself and the rest of our family. So I did the work. I practiced everything I preach and teach. I not only found healing, but I found incredible transformation and even purpose.

It wasn't easy. I cried a lot the first few months after Tristin died. As I mentioned, he died November 14 and Christmas was just around the corner. I allowed myself to feel the emotions and that was a big part of healing. Again, I can't say it enough: we have been taught to avoid and distract from feeling our pain. We turn to food, alcohol, work—whatever we can do to not deal with or feel the pain. Feeling pain is the path to freedom. Sadly, most of us aren't taught that. I continued to do the work, to meditate daily and practice yoga. I avoided alcohol, as I knew that would just make things worse. I have never struggled with alcohol, but there were times in my life where I definitely turned to it as a means of avoiding my pain or numbing it. For me in the past, extreme exercise seemed to be my outlet or distraction tool. We all have a vehicle we choose to escape dealing with our shit. Some vehicles are just much more detrimental to our health than others. At the end of the day, we are all addicted to something.

In addition to my spiritual practices, I took a new action approach through the Grief Recovery Method® a program I took through the Grief Recovery Institute. When I finally learned how to find completion to the pain from my past experiences, I found freedom. Freedom from the pain. This was a significant shift for me. I had no idea that a person could go through something so heartbreaking and come out of it with acceptance, peace, and even gratitude.

At this point I knew I had to teach others to have this same experience, and I was eager to learn more about trauma and addictions. I eventually got certified to teach that very program that helped me find freedom.

Chapter 8

I had reached out to the addiction treatment centre that Tristin attended to inform them of his passing. One of the staff who he was close to attended his celebration of life and had also invited me to attend a sweat lodge ceremony. I was touched by this offer and the experience. I arrived at the Treatment Centre and walked up to the front doors, and as I did so, what came out of my mouth was, "I would really like to work here just a few days a week," and so the seed was planted. The other thing that happens when you do the work, besides healing, is you open yourself up to opportunities and even miracles.

On January 16, 2020, I started working in a casual position at that very same addiction treatment centre, and stayed on staff for 2 years. During my last year there, my own Business grew so much and demand for my programs and services left very little time to work at the treatment centre, so I decided to shift my attention and focus solely on my own clients. I am very grateful for the time I was able to be of service there.

In March of 2020 I started an addiction certification program and also started to study trauma. I became even more aware of how we as a society have created all the mental health and addiction concerns we are experiencing today. I started to deepen my awareness and understanding of multi-generational trauma, and more importantly I became more aware of how unaware most of society is.

The clients I have met at the addiction treatment centre are some of the most talented, friendly, loving people I have ever met. Every one of them has experienced trauma. Trauma doesn't discriminate, nor does addiction. I have seen people of all ages, all genders, all ethnicities from all career paths in treatment for drugs or alcohol. I have even met people who work in the health industry themselves who have enrolled in treatment.

"Not all trauma leads to addiction, but all addiction stems from trauma." I am pretty sure I first heard this from Dr. Gabor Maté. After working at the addiction treatment centre for almost two years, I can 100 percent agree.

We all have unresolved grief. We all have experienced trauma, and most of us are addicted to something that helps us to distract from the pain, the discomfort and/

or the unmet hopes dreams and expectations we have for our lives.

The truth is that more shit is going to happen—and it did!

Spring of 2020 brought a global pandemic that brought an abundance of trauma and grief that has drastically caused a significant rise in statistics for mental health, addictions, suicide, and overdose.

In July of 2020, I officially began offering grief/trauma coaching through my existing business, Empowered Life. I had been leading workshops and various personal development programs for a few years by then, but I finally felt like I had truly found my calling. In spring of 2021 I started my year-long training with Dr. Gabor Maté to become certified in his Compassionate Inquiry program. I also registered in a yoga therapy certification program, and have a list of a few other trainings and certifications I plan to complete. Healing is a lifelong journey, there is no destination.

I have worked with clients one on one and in group settings, both in person and online. It continues to bring more awareness and healing into my life, and it is highly rewarding to see others move from suffering to empowerment. I have been blessed to support so many people through incredible healing journeys and transformation.

I found my purpose. I thank Tristin every day for this beautiful gift.

Awareness is half the battle. You can't fix, change, or improve what you are not aware of. My deeper awareness and understanding of trauma, multi-generational trauma, and grief have brought incredible clarity and insight into my own life and changed my view of society and of life in general.

Many people are completely blind to the fact that they have grief or trauma. I have had several people sign up for programs and tell me, "I don't feel like I have a lot of grief, but I feel like I should do this program." Halfway through, they share how surprised they are about how much they misunderstood what grief and trauma actually are. They also usually come up with a long list of unresolved grief and trauma. Then we start the healing and transformation process.

I had one client halfway through a program send me messages that read, "I just want you to know that this loss history graph is horseshit and I hate it but I'm going to do it anyway even though I don't fucking want to anymore," followed by a laughing face emoji. Those were my client's exact words. When finished, she was very happy she followed through, and in fact signed up to go through the program again and eventually became a certified facilitator of my program.

Every client, when they have finished the program, has also said they are so glad they did it.

I have also had a few clients who have said they found more healing and recovery in these programs than years of working with a therapist. The key: treat the root cause rather than the symptoms. Everything roots to emotion. Anxiety, depression, anger, violence, isolation, and similar behaviours are symptoms of trauma and unresolved grief.

Healing and recovery come from action. By action I don't mean talking about your feelings or emotions, although that is an important part.

First you have to identify what actually needs to be healed, all of it, right back from childhood. Once you identify the events or experiences, you need to tap into the emotion experienced during those times, the emotions and emotional statements need to be verbalized, and, most importantly, they need to be heard.

There is nothing worse than pouring out your heart and soul to someone only to have them say something like, "Oh yeah, I lost my dad, too," or, "I know how you feel," or, "He is in a better place now," or, "Be strong, just give it time." How many times have you heard that? Have you said it? I have.

For the person expressing their grief, this is like finally having the courage to pour your emotions out and then basically having to swallow them back down because the response makes it seem like your grief doesn't matter or it's not a big deal. It is a big deal. It is a very big deal. What really needs to happen after sharing your emotions is for someone to simply say, "Thank you for sharing that. I can't imagine how you feel. I am here to listen, anytime." That is it. No comparing stories, no comments in attempt to make the person feel better.

How many times have you handed someone a tissue when they are crying, or swooped in to hug them. I bet more times than you can count. Although your intentions are good, you are actually sending a message that says, *Don't cry, don't feel the pain.* We reinforce the avoid-and-distract method.

We have experienced this as children when we fell and hurt ourselves, and have done it to our children when they fell. It is one of two things. It is either, "Get up, don't cry, you are OK," or we swoop in and rub the knee or head and hug and kiss. Again, although the intentions are good, it teaches "don't feel the pain." It is all we are ever taught. Don't feel the pain, don't feel sad, don't feel bad. No wonder we have so many mental health and addiction concerns in this world.

I can tell you from my own experience and from the many clients I have worked with that healing and transformation is possible. You have to *do the work*, and you have to do it for the rest of your life.

Change is when *one or a few things* are different. Transformation is when *everything* is different. I continue to do the work and I continue to transform. Doing the work means undoing all that we learned that doesn't serve us, and learning to rewire ourselves to approach life in a new and better way. It doesn't mean you won't ever feel pain or sadness again; I promise you, you will.

Magic and miracles happen when you do the work. I have experienced it and I continue to manifest all sorts of incredible opportunities and experiences.

Chapter 9

Tristin continues to guide me on this journey of serving my purpose. He brings me ideas and inspirations during my meditations. I truly feel like we are co-creating this amazing life that continues to unfold daily.

Through this new connection I have with him, the seed he planted in my heart and soul early in 2021 was the idea for a new all-encompassing program to truly teach people to overcome not only their traumas and grief, but to also identify and change limiting beliefs, learn to shift from fear-based living to heart-based living, discover how to find more balance and alignment, and learn how to truly create and attract abundance.

June 2021 saw the launch of my new four-week online program: Empowered Transformation. That seed Tristin planted not only grew into this program, but it sprouted a second bloom, the facilitator program that launched in the fall of 2021. There are now over twenty trained facilitators sharing this program worldwide.

This program has grown faster than I anticipated. It has changed many lives and it has brought me so much joy to see others experience such empowered healing.

My pain has turned into a movement of people helping people. This gift came at the cost of my son's life. I thank him every day for the suffering and sacrifices he experienced that have allowed so many others to heal. I can't think of a more beautiful gift.

In case you are wondering, yes, I miss him every single day. I think about him as soon as I wake up and before I go to sleep and several times in between. I still have moments where I feel sad and shed some tears; however, I am not suffering. I am not stuck in pain. I have sad moments and I also have many fond memories and new experiences with Tristin, just in new ways.

I also, in a way, feel even closer to him now. I receive signs and messages from him all the time. Strange things happen in my house: lights flashing, objects moving, I "hear" him in my mediations and often during my yoga practice. All my ideas and inspirations for my programs, my workshops, come from him. He shows up in photos—I have quite the magnificent collection of photos with incredible orbs and energy. I have also found connection to other spiritual guides and more loved ones passed.

I have received profound and very personal messages from Tristin, channelled through gifted intuitives, including one session in August 2021. I was sharing the details of my reading with Kaylee, Tristin's girlfriend. My friend Sheila, who was channelling him had said, "He is showing me chocolate milk." I chuckled because he loved chocolate milk, so much that he would even ask me to bring him chocolate milk when I would visit him in treatment.

Kaylee laughed when I told her and said he would buy twenty single-serve chocolate milk bottles at a time, he loved it so much.

Prior to my conversation with Kaylee, I had asked Tristin to give me a sign letting me know he was still around. About thirty minutes after my conversation with Kaylee, I went to our local grocery store. I came around a corner and there in front of me was a giant display of single-serve chocolate milk. I am sure you can imagine the smile it brought to my face. There are so many more like this.

We don't have to move on from the loved ones we have lost. We can move forward with them, just in a new and different way. When you figure this out, a beautiful new relationship is born.

I had an incredible opportunity in June of 2021 to name a cottage after Tristin at a very special new retreat centre that opened up just north of Edmonton. Due to COVID, I had to reschedule a retreat I had planned; however, the venue was unable to accommodate new dates, as they had decided to close permanently. A friend told me about a new retreat location opening up, so I decided to check it out. I tell you, it was divinely orchestrated! Riverside Acres retreat was set to open July of 2021. It was created to be a healing space inspired by a young girl who lost her life to suicide. This young girl's aunt and uncle are the owners. This magnificent place has six cottages, and an idea came forth to name the cottages after people who had left this earth too soon. When I found this out, I asked if there was still a cottage available for naming. Lo and behold, there was still a few available. I didn't have to give it a second thought. Karen, the aunt/owner, and I quickly became friends. I have hosted a few retreats and workshops out there, and Tristin's cottage and five others are available for anyone wanting to spend some time in nature healing, relaxing, and enjoying life. It has blossomed into the most beautiful and magical piece of heaven on earth!

The photos above are from various times over the summer of 2021. These are a few of many photos that capture the amazing spirit energy that surrounds this magnificent place. This is not only Tristin's energy, but the energy of the other five men who left this earth too soon.[1] All photos from this book can be viewed in colour on the Empowered Life website.

---

1   Riverside Acres Retreat: www.riversideacres.net

Chapter 10

If you take anything away from this book, I hope it is the following valuable life lessons:

1. Tomorrow is never guaranteed.
2. You have no control over anyone or anything outside of you.
3. We all have past experiences to heal.
4. Triggers are something to be grateful for; they are simply sensations in the body, trying to get your attention to direct you to what needs to be healed.
5. Your body is full of wisdom, more wisdom than your mind. Get out of your head, get into your body.
6. The definition of guilt is "with intention to cause harm." If your intentions are good, and you are doing your best, you have *nothing* to feel guilty for.
7. Most of our *feelings* are actually *perceptions*. Our perceptions are often inaccurate.

8. Pain is the path to freedom; avoiding the pain is suffering. There is never freedom in suffering.
9. The best way to help heal your kids is to heal yourself.
10. Healing is possible, *if you do the work.*
11. You only know what you know, and when you know better, you do better.

I found a song on my laptop, in my downloads a few months after Tristin had passed. I had forgotten about it. It was a song he had made up on the spot when we were driving. He had recently completed his first round of treatment at the addiction centre. We had gone to a meditation class and we were driving home. He started singing, and it was at this point I realized he was quite a good freestyle rapper. I said to him, "OK, do another one and I will record it on my phone." So he found a beat to play on his phone, I hit record on my phone, and he started to rap.

It was from this song that I first got the tag of "mom. calm."[2]

---

[2]   mom.calm: https://youtu.be/MnGF8do4icY

In loving memory, Tristin Snell, July 24, 1997–Nov 14, 2019. May you rest in peace and may your light continue to shine down upon us.

As your mom, I may have given you life,
but truly it is you who gave me life.
There is no greater gift a person could give or receive.

All photos can be viewed in colour on my website
along with information on my follow up book
https://empoweredlifenow.net/my-books

Since publishing this book, my spiritual journey has led me into Mediumship and the experience warrants a follow up book about moving from empowerment to enlightenment. I continue to facilitate programs and trainings and I also offer coaching in the areas of Trauma/ Grief Recovery and Spiritual Empowerment. Jan 2022, I began offering LIVE weekly channeling sessions in my Facebook group. I have had many souls passed come to me with messages for loved ones still on earth. I believe Trisitn is bringing them to me. I am excited to see where this path takes me. I will be sure to include the details in my follow up book.

If you are interested in the free, live, weekly channeling, join the Facebook group here:
https://www.facebook.com/groups/887016645251334

Follow me for all the details on the release of my next book and for a full list of online programs and services available.

Fb – Empowered Life with Kim Wilkinson
https://www.facebook.com/kimwilkinsoncoaching

Main website:
https://empoweredlifenow.net

Online School
https://empoweredlife.teachable.com

Email:
kimwilkinsoncoaching@gmail.com